Shifting Sands

Contents

Features

WORD BUILDER

Which would you rather eat, *desert* or *dessert*? Turn to page 5 and never order sand at a restaurant again!

FAST FACTS

Just what do camels carry in their humps? You might be surprised! Find out on page 11.

WHAT'S YOUR OPINION?

Many deserts have been turned into farmland by the use of pipes that provide water. Turn to page 12 for more.

IN FOCUS

A successful exploration not only reaches its destination but also gets back again. Turn to page 23 to learn about two explorers who got it only half right.

SITESEEING · PEOPLE & PLACES ·

How is oil made?

Visit www.infosteps.co.uk
for more about DESERT RESOURCES.

What Is a Desert?

Planet Earth has many climates. These range from hot and wet to cold and dry. Deserts are created by climates that have dry winds and little rain. When we think of deserts, we often think of very hot places, but deserts aren't always hot. The Gobi Desert in Asia for example can get very cold.

Desert areas get less than 25 centimetres of rain each year. However, some years it may rain much more. This rain often comes in the form of a **downpour**. Some years it may not rain at all!

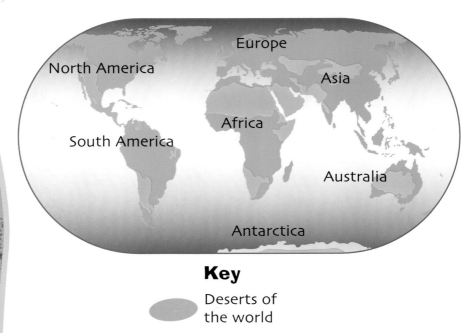

Key

Deserts of the world

It is so cold and dry in Antarctica that it rarely rains or even snows. Antarctica is often called a **polar desert**.

WORD BUILDER

One way of remembering the correct spelling of *desert* is to think about whether you would like a second helping of sand or ice cream! The *dessert* we eat has two "helpings" of the letter *s*.

Desert Life

Features of Desert Plants

Plants have a tough life in a desert. The soil is usually poor and there is little water. Days can be very hot and nights can be very cold.

Desert plants have special ways of living in this difficult climate. Many plants have thick fleshy stems and roots that store water. If they have leaves, the leaves are usually very small. Some plants such as cacti have spines or prickles that shade the plants' stems and help protect them from being eaten by animals.

Rainfall in a desert is rare. When it does rain, plants quickly spring to life, growing leaves, flowering and setting seed within days.

In some deserts an underground river comes to the surface to form an **oasis**. These waterholes are important to the people and animals that live in desert regions.

Features of Desert Creatures

Heat and lack of water are problems for desert animals too. Many animals such as the kangaroo rat are **nocturnal** to avoid the heat. During the daytime heat they stay underground where it is cool. Other animals rest in the shade.

Some small animals get most or even all of the moisture they need from the leaves and fruit of plants. Meat eaters get a lot of moisture from the animals they eat. However, many desert animals also stay near water.

American Southwest Desert Animals

Key

1 black-collared lizard
2 cactus wren
3 bobcat
4 tortoise
5 grey fox
6 horned lizard
7 rattlesnake
8 roadrunner
9 kangaroo rat
10 cottontail rabbit

Ships of the Desert

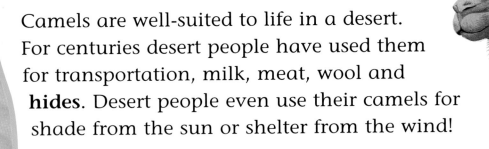

Camels are well-suited to life in a desert. For centuries desert people have used them for transportation, milk, meat, wool and **hides**. Desert people even use their camels for shade from the sun or shelter from the wind!

Camels have two sets of long eyelashes that help keep sand out of their eyes. Their broad flat feet stop them from sinking into sand. They can easily survive for up to seven days with little or no food or water. When water is available however, they can drink huge amounts.

An Arabian camel, or dromedary, has only one hump.

Bactrian camels such as this one from the Gobi Desert have two humps.

FAST FACTS

A camel stores fat not water in its humps and can live on this fat for a long time. But when a camel has to live on its hump fat, its humps get smaller and fall sideways! When the camel gets food and rest, its humps grow large again.

From Sand to Farmland

People can produce crops in even the driest areas of the world by using **irrigation**. Thousands of years ago people built dams to collect water. They dug open canals to take this water to their crops. Open canals weren't ideal because water was lost due to **evaporation**.

People still build dams to collect water, but now they use pipes to carry water instead of open canals. Pipes can carry large amounts of water over long distances. Sprinklers then spray the water onto thirsty land, turning desert areas into farmland.

WHAT'S YOUR OPINION?

Some people believe that deserts should be left as they are and not irrigated because they are a fragile environment. Other people believe the need to grow food is more important. What do you think?

Parker Dam on the Colorado River in Arizona, USA

Salt Lake City in Utah, USA is surrounded by desert.

People of the Desert

Life in a desert depends on water. In the past many people who lived in deserts were **nomads** who travelled long distances from waterhole to waterhole. They hunted or herded animals and traded goods with other tribes.

Today many of the world's deserts are criss-crossed with power lines and irrigation channels. The people who live in these deserts no longer have to travel in search of water. With water and power even large cities can exist in the desert.

Las Vegas, Nevada, USA is a city in a desert.

The Bedouin people are desert nomads. For centuries they wandered the deserts of the Middle East and northern Africa with their herds of camels, sheep, goats or horses. Today many Bedouins have settled in towns, but some still choose the wandering way of life.

Portrait of a Desert

Living in the Climate

The Gobi Desert is in Asia. It is a cool desert which gets warm in summer. The winters are very cold. Rain does not fall often, but there are freshwater ponds that are fed by mountain streams and underground rivers.

Most of the people who live in the Gobi Desert are nomads who keep horses, camels, cattle, sheep and goats. They live in felt tents called gers. The felt is made by beating and rolling wet sheep's wool.

Not much has changed in centuries for the people of the Gobi Desert. Their main job is still animal herding.

The insides of the nomads' tents are richly decorated. Guests are always given a warm welcome.

Gobi Desert, Mongolia

Shifting Sand Dunes

The sand dunes of the Gobi Desert are spreading, blown by strong winds. This process is called **desertification**. Most scientists think that desertification is caused by too many animals eating what little grass is available and by people cutting down trees. Without grass and tree roots to hold the sandy soil together, it is easily blown by the wind. People are now planting trees to help slow the spread of the desert.

In some parts of the Gobi Desert very strong winds produce the largest sand dunes in the world. Some of these sand dunes are over 300 metres high!

Sandstorms blowing from the Gobi Desert have become common in northern China, reaching as far as the city of Beijing.

Gobi Desert
Beijing

Beneath the Surface

Deserts often have valuable rocks and minerals beneath their surfaces. The deserts of southern Africa are mined for diamonds. The Australian Desert contains gems called opals. The deserts of Saudi Arabia are drilled for oil.

Along the Arizona-Utah border in the United States the Navajo people collect a mineral called turquoise. They polish it until it is a beautiful sky-blue colour. The turquoise can then be made into jewellery. Many people live and work in desert areas, finding these hidden treasures.

Coober Pedy is a town in the Australian Desert that is famous for its opal mines. Temperatures there can reach 50 degrees Celsius so many people live in cool underground houses!

An underground home

How is oil made?
Visit **www.infosteps.co.uk**
for more about **DESERT RESOURCES.**

SITESEEING
PEOPLE & PLACES

Desert Crossings

In the past, people tried to cross deserts for many reasons. Some were looking for riches. Some were looking for new trading routes. Some wanted to cross a desert because it had never been done before.

Crossing a desert today is still a challenge even though people usually use four-wheel-drive vehicles instead of camels. People who attempt to cross a desert must be carefully prepared with maps, water, food, fuel and a phone or radio so they can call for help if they need it.

IN FOCUS

In 1860 John Wills and Robert Burke set out to find a route across the desert from the south to the north of Australia. When they finally reached Flinders River, their turnaround point, they discovered they did not have enough supplies left for the return trip. Burke and Wills got weaker and weaker. They even ate their two remaining camels but that didn't save them. They both died from lack of food before they could make their way back home.

Australia

John Wills

Robert Burke

Hidden Treasures

For centuries treasure lay hidden in Egypt, completely covered by the shifting sands of the Sahara Desert. It was not until the 1800s that the Valley of the Kings was discovered.

Many kings of ancient Egypt were buried with their belongings in the Valley of the Kings. They were placed in tombs with false doors and empty rooms to fool robbers. However, robbers were not often fooled—the treasure in most ancient tombs was stolen a long time ago!

King Tutankhamen's tomb was discovered in 1922. Unlike most ancient tombs, it had not been robbed of its treasures. King Tutankhamen had been buried in a solid gold coffin!

Kings' tombs are also found in Giza, Egypt.

Sand Painting

The Navajo people of the American Southwest use coloured sand to make paintings for healing **ceremonies** and as a form of art.

In a healing ceremony the medicine man, or singer, creates a sand painting on the floor. The patient then sits in the centre of the painting. As the ceremony is completed, all the coloured sand is swept away. Sand painting is also used as an art form. Many of these paintings show different views of life.

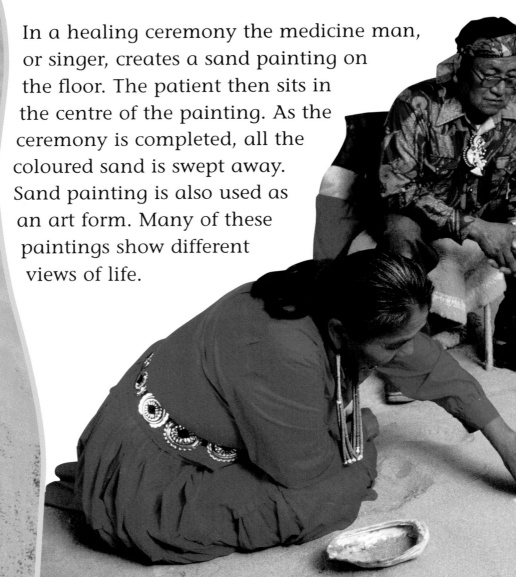

Mandala sand paintings are made in Tibet from millions of grains of coloured sand, carefully arranged over days or even weeks. Once a painting is finished the sand is swept up and poured into nearby water.

Desert Fun

Deserts can be great fun. They are special areas with plants and animals that are not found in other places.

People who like adventure can go hiking and climbing. They can ride camels or horses on long treks in a desert. There are places in deserts where people who enjoy going fast can ride dune buggies and dirt bikes. People can even sail "boats" on desert sand flats. However, some people prefer to sit and watch the birds or the setting sun.

Look after ⟨...⟩ ⟨...⟩ironment. When you
visit a deser⟨...⟩ ⟨...⟩ly photos and leave only
footprints!

Glossary

ceremonies – special actions and words performed on important occasions

desertification – the way in which farmland becomes desert over time

downpour – a heavy fall of rain. In very dry areas this can quickly cause flooding.

evaporation – the way in which heated water turns to steam

hides – animal skins used to make goods such as clothing or leather objects

irrigation – a system of pipes or canals that bring water to areas of dry land

nocturnal – an animal that sleeps during the day and is active at night

nomads – people who wander, usually within one area, living in homes that are easily moved

oasis – an area in a desert where underground water flows to the surface

polar desert – an area around either the North or the South Pole where there is little or no rain or snow. These areas are among the most difficult to live in on Earth.

Index

Discussion Starters

1 People, plants and animals all live in deserts. What are some of the problems they face? How do you think they overcome these difficulties?

2 There are several different types of climates in the world. Can you make a list of those you know? Which climate would you most like to live in? Which places in the world have difficult climates to live in?

3 In the past most of the people who lived in deserts were nomads. Why do you think this was true? What has changed about deserts today? What has stayed the same?